Table o

MW00612694

Jerry Baker
America's / Master Gardener®

Introduction

In my 30+ years of gardening, one thing I've learned is that beautiful, attractive and healthy yards and gardens (yardens) don't just happen. They are the result of the 3 P's – Pride, Patience, and Persistence – along with knowing what to do and when to do it.

This booklet tells you what to do and when to do it by taking you step-by-step through the growing season. You'll learn how to have the greenest grass, prettiest flowers, tastiest fruits and vegetables, and healthiest plants on your side of the fence with a minimum of time, effort and expense. And best of all, I'll show you how to do it using common, everyday items that you've already got around the house.

If you have a yardening question, why don't you call me **"On The Garden Line"** Saturday mornings from 8:00 a.m. - 10:00 a.m. EST on your local Mutual Broadcasting Station. The toll-free number is **1-800-634-3881.**

Also, for more comprehensive information, please refer to one of my other full size books:

Plants Are Still Like People
Jerry Baker's Flowering Garden
The Impatient Gardener
Fast, Easy Vegetable Garden
Jerry Baker's Lawn Book
Happy, Healthy House Plants

or pick up a copy of **America's Gardening Newsletter, "On The Garden Line®,"** which is also jam-packed with timely tips, tricks and tonics on lawn, garden and plant care.

Many a home yardener thinks so little of the need to do a serious job of spring cleaning that they just skip it, and go on to what they think are other, more important chores. That, my friends, is the biggest mistake you can make if you want your yarden to survive and thrive.

So the first thing you should do is rake, blow, vacuum and sweep every area of your yarden clean so that a raccoon could eat off of the dirt without washing its food. No kidding!

The reason for this thorough cleaning is that winter debris hides and houses dozens upon dozens of problems in the form of insects and disease. Until it is removed, you're only asking for trouble! So, remember Jerry's First Commandment – **Cleanliness is next to Godliness when it comes to yarden care!**

America's Master Gardener

AREA
Map

To begin, locate your Area on the map and write it in the appropriate blank on the following page. Do the same for the average minimum temperature, average number of growing days, when spring begins and when fall begins in your Area.

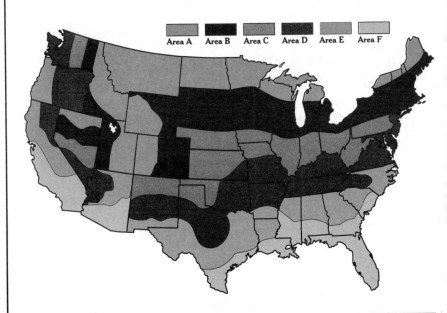

Area	Avg. Min. Temp. (°F)	Avg. No. Growing Days	Spring Begins (Approx.)	Fall Begins (Approx.)
A	-50 to -30°	145	May 15	Sept. 30
B	-30 to -10°	175	April 15	Oct. 31
C	-10 to 10°	185	April 15	Oct. 31
D	10 to 30°	220	April 1	Oct. 31
E	30 to 40°	250	March 15	Nov. 15
F	Above 40°	320	Jan. 15	Dec. 15

Once you fill in the appropriate blanks below, take a blue sticker and a green sticker and place them on your daily calendar on the date that spring begins in your Area. By this date, you should complete your preliminary cleanup, soil build-up and preparation chores, and you should begin cleaning and greening up your yarden. To do so, you should apply a "Clean Up" and "Green Up" Tonic which I'll tell you about later.

After you initially clean and green up your yarden in spring, you should then apply a "Clean Up" Tonic every 2 weeks, and a "Green Up" Tonic every 3 weeks for the rest of the growing season. So you don't forget, take blue reminder stickers and place them on your calendar at 2 week intervals until fall begins in your Area; do the same with green reminder stickers, only place them at 3 week intervals. If you start my program anytime during the growing season, don't worry; simply place a blue and green sticker on the date when you first apply a "Clean Up" and a "Green Up" Tonic, and then place blue and green stickers at 2 week and 3 week intervals respectively. That's all there is to it.

Area Summary

My Area Is: _____

Avg. Min. Temp. _____

Avg. No. Grow. Days _____

Spring Begins: _____

Fall Begins: _____

SAFETY

When applying any tonic or other material to your yarden, ALWAYS THINK SAFETY FIRST, by following these simple steps:

Step 1: Before using any sprayer, read all of the directions on the sprayer jar.

Step 2: Before applying any material with a sprayer, "test drive" it using water. This allows you to see exactly how it works and what it will do.

Step 3: Dress sensibly; don't wear shorts or a bathing suit when spraying! Wear gloves (plastic throwaways will do) and a hat if you're spraying at or above eye level. Also, wear sun or safety glasses when spraying, and place a bandanna over your mouth, since an unexpected breeze can blow the spray back into your face.

Step 4: Measure the proper amount of tonic or material, then apply it according to the directions.

Step 5: Set aside all measuring spoons and cups for use only in your yarden.

Step 6: To prevent drifting of spray to non-target areas, never spray any tonic or material on a windy day.

Step 7: For maximum effectiveness – not to mention less wear and tear on you – spray in the cool of the day.

Step 8: When you are finished, thoroughly clean and drain your sprayer with a mild solution of soap and water.

Step 9: Never pour unused tonics or yarden material down the drain; dispose of them properly.

Step 10: Always store all yarden materials out of the reach of children, preferably in a locked cabinet.

Step 11: Always keep materials in their original containers and never remove the label. Also, never mix 'n' match different yarden materials.

Step 12: Always dispose of partially filled or empty containers properly, as recommended on the label. Do not burn them!

Step 13: ALWAYS READ ALL OF THE DIRECTIONS ON LABELS, STICKERS AND PACKAGES, AND I MEAN ALL OF THEM!

Don't take anything for granted, don't take any shortcuts, and read the entire label before you take the cap off. Then mix only at the recommended rate or less, never more.

REMEMBER, IT'S ALWAYS BETTER TO BE SAFE, THAN SORRY!

SAFETY TIPS

- Read all directions before applying any material.
- Mix spray materials exactly as specified.
- Spray in the cool of the day.
- Never spray on a windy day.
- Dress sensibly.
- Thoroughly clean and dry your sprayers when finished.
- Store all yarden materials in a locked area out of the reach of children.

☑ INVENTORY

Before you apply anything to your yarden, you need to know how big it is so that you can determine exactly how much tonic and other material you will need to efficiently, effectively and economically cover your growing areas.

PREPARING YOUR INVENTORY:

1 First, measure the perimeter of your yard, including your home, garage and/or storage shed, driveway, walkways, decks, lawn, trees, shrubs, evergreens, flower beds and vegetable garden, jotting down notes as you go along.

2 Then, using your notes, draw the shape of your property according to scale on the charts on the following pages. Also note which direction is north.

3 Next, draw your home, any other buildings, structures, driveways, walkways, and any recreation or use areas onto the charts.

4 Now, draw in all of your major trees, shrubs, evergreens, groundcovers, flower beds and vegetable garden on the charts, using the symbols provided.

5 Finally, calculate your total yarden square footage in the Work Area on the next page. Once you complete these calculations, you've got a permanent record of your outdoor living area.

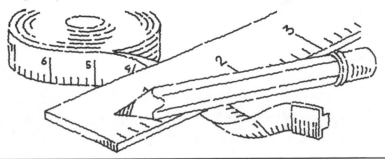

INVENTORY
Work Area

LAWN

Front Length _____ Ft. x Width _____ = _____ Sq. Ft.

Back Length _____ Ft. x Width _____ = _____ Sq. Ft.

Side Length _____ Ft. x Width _____ = _____ Sq. Ft.

Side Length _____ Ft. x Width _____ = _____ Sq. Ft.

TREES, SHRUBS & EVERGREENS

Number of Trees _____

Bed 1 Length _____ Ft. x Width _____ = _____ Sq. Ft.

Bed 2 Length _____ Ft. x Width _____ = _____ Sq. Ft.

FLOWER BEDS

Bed 1 Length _____ Ft. x Width _____ = _____ Sq. Ft.

Bed 2 Length _____ Ft. x Width _____ = _____ Sq. Ft.

VEGETABLE GARDEN

Length _____ Ft. x Width _____ = _____ Sq. Ft.

SUMMARY

Lawn _____ Sq. Ft.   Flowers _____ Sq. Ft.

Trees, etc. _____ Sq. Ft.   Vegetables _____ Sq. Ft.

TOTAL YARDEN SQ. FT. _____

INVENTORY
Chart

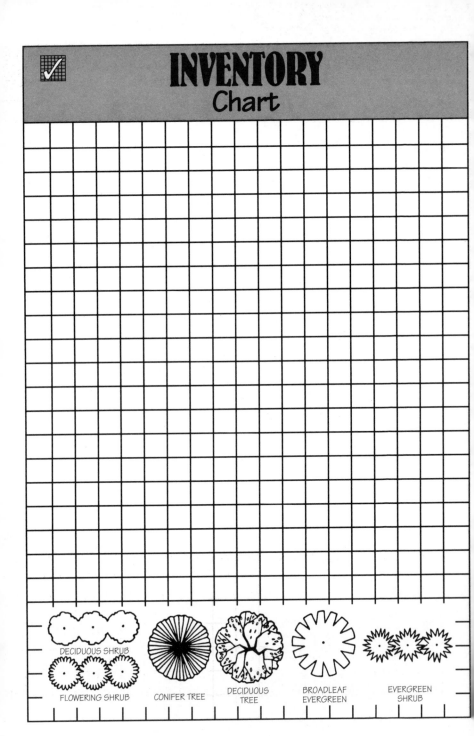

DECIDUOUS SHRUB

FLOWERING SHRUB

CONIFER TREE

DECIDUOUS TREE

BROADLEAF EVERGREEN

EVERGREEN SHRUB

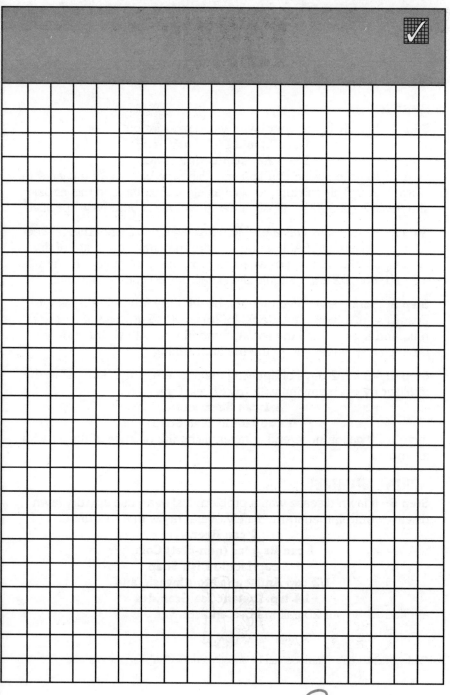

America's / Master Gardener®

LAWNS

SPRING

Step 1: Initially bathe your lawn with a mixture of:

1 cup Liquid Dish Soap,* and
1 cup Antiseptic Mouthwash

in your 20 gallon hose-end sprayer, filling the balance of the jar with warm water. This mixture, as well as all of the others in this booklet, should cover 2,500 sq. ft. of yarden area unless otherwise specified.

Step 2: If crabgrass was a problem last year, use a pre-emerge weed control containing TEAM. If you use dry material, add 1 cup of dry laundry soap to the bag of weed control, mix and spread. If you use a liquid, add 1/2 cup of liquid dish soap per 20 gallons of water.

Step 3: Spring lawn feeding must be with dry food. Add 3 lbs. of Epsom salts to your favorite 50 lb. (or 2500 sq. ft.) bag of fertilizer, mix, and apply at half the recommended rate with your hand-held broadcast spreader set on the medium setting.

Step 4: Within 2 days of applying the above mixture, jump start the fertilizer by overspraying with my Snack Tonic:

1 can Beer, and
1 cup Liquid Dish Soap

in your 20 gallon hose-end sprayer, filling the balance of the jar with ammonia.

SPRING/SUMMER

Step 5: If lawn disease was a problem last year, use any dry lawn disease control, then immediately overspray with a mixture of:

1 can Beer,
1 can Regular (non-diet) Cola,
1/2 cup Liquid Dish Soap,
1/2 cup Antiseptic Mouthwash, and
1/4 tsp. Instant Tea Granules

applied with your 20 gallon hose-end sprayer.

*Baby or children's shampoo can be substituted for dish soap throughout.

Step 6: After your initial spring feeding, feed your lawn every 3 weeks, in the morning, for the rest of the growing season with my All Season "Green Up" Tonic:

1 can Beer,

1 cup Ammonia,

1/2 cup Liquid Dish Soap,

1/2 cup Liquid Lawn Food, and

1/2 cup Molasses or Corn Syrup

applied with your 20 gallon hose-end sprayer.

NOTE: If grass clippings are not picked up, overspray your lawn once a month with a mixture of:

1 can Regular (non-diet) Cola

1/2 cup Liquid Dish Soap

1/4 cup Ammonia

in your 20 gallon hose-end sprayer, filling the balance of the jar with warm water. Also overspray your compost pile with this mixture after adding new yarden fodder.

Step 7: Clean plants are healthy plants, so to discourage insects and prevent disease, bathe your lawn every 2 weeks, right after you mow, for the rest of the growing season with my All Season "Clean Up" Tonic:

1 cup Liquid Dish Soap,

1 cup Chewing Tobacco Juice*, and

1 cup Antiseptic Mouthwash,

in your 20 gallon hose-end sprayer, filling the balance of the jar with warm water.

*Chewing tobacco juice is made by placing 3 fingers of chewing tobacco in an old nylon stocking and soaking it in a gallon of hot water until the mixture is dark brown.

Step 8: If soil insect control is necessary, add DURSBAN at the recommended rate to the Step 7 mixture.

Step 9: Proper watering is a must, although it is a job that cannot be defined. I recommend watering before 2:00 p.m.; anytime between 5:00 a.m. and 8:00 a.m. is best to minimize evaporation loss.

FALL

Step 10: Kill weeds between September 1 and October 1 on a warm (between 70-80°F), sunny day. Pre-wash your lawn using your 20 gallon hose-end sprayer with **1 cup of liquid dish soap** added, filling the balance of the jar with warm water. Now mix only the amount of weed killer that you need in a different 20 gallon hose-end sprayer. If you use liquid weed & feed, follow these same steps. If you use dry weed & feed, wash your lawn and apply it while the lawn is still damp.

Step 11: As a final feeding in fall, add 3 pounds of Epsom salts to your favorite 50 lb. (or 2500 sq. ft.) bag of fertilizer, mix, and apply at half the recommended rate with your hand-held broadcast spreader set on the medium setting. If you apply Weed & Feed, only use 1 lb. Epsom salts.

Step 12: Within 2 days of applying the above mixture, overspray with a mixture of:

1 can Beer, and
1/2 cup Liquid Dish Soap

in your 20 gallon hose-end sprayer, filling the balance of the jar with ammonia.

Step 13: To control insects, spray the infected areas with 1 cup liquid dish soap in your 20 gallon hose-end sprayer, filling the balance of the jar with warm water. Then apply DURSBAN at the recommended rate.

Step 14: Mow your lawn until it stops growing, then drop the blade one notch and mow one more time.

Step 15: Rake and remove all fallen leaves, shred them with your lawn mower, and add them to your compost pile or garden area. Never let fallen leaves cover your lawn over the winter.

Step 16: Drain the oil and gas from your lawn mower and put it away until next spring.

LAWN TIPS

- Always wear your golf shoes when working in your yarden.
- Water before 2:00 p.m.; between 5:00 a.m. and 8:00 a.m. is best.
- Pick up all grass clippings (use them as a garden mulch).
- Apply weed controls between 1:00 p.m. and 3:00 p.m. on a bright, sunny day.
- Apply disease controls after 1:00 p.m.
- Mow after 7:00 p.m.
- Mow only with sharp blades.

TREES,
Shrubs & Evergreens

SPRING

Step 1: As soon as you can, wash down this group with a mixture of:
1 cup Liquid Dish Soap,
1 cup Chewing Tobacco Juice, and
1 cup Antiseptic Mouthwash
in your 10 gallon hose-end sprayer, filling the balance of the jar with warm water.

Step 2: Feed this group with a dry mix of:
25 lbs. Garden Food,
1 lb. Sugar, and
1/2 lb. Epsom salts

Feed your trees by drilling holes out at the weep line, 8 to 10" deep, 18 to 24" apart in 2' circles. Fill the holes with 2 tbsp. of the above mixture; sprinkle the remainder over the soil.

Feed your shrubs and evergreens by spreading the above mixture with your handheld broadcast spreader set on the medium setting.

Step 3: Overspray this dry feeding with a mixture of:
1 can Beer,
1 cup Liquid Lawn Food,
1/2 cup Liquid Dish Soap, and
1/2 cup Ammonia
in your 10 gallon hose-end sprayer, filling the balance of the jar with regular (non-diet) cola.

Step 4: If above ground bugs are a problem, apply a mixture of:
Fruit Tree Spray at half the recommended rate,
1/2 cup Liquid Dish Soap,
1/2 cup Chewing Tobacco Juice, and
1/2 cup Antiseptic Mouthwash
in your 10 gallon hose-end sprayer, filling the balance of the jar with warm water. Apply any such spray after the sun starts to go down.

Step 5: If you see signs of soil insect damage or activity, replace the fruit tree spray in the Step 4 mixture with DURSBAN added at the recommended rate.

SUMMER

Step 6: Feeding should be kept to a mild liquid diet, so every 3 weeks, feed this group with my All Season "Green Up" Tonic:

1 can Beer,
1 cup Ammonia,
1/2 cup Liquid Dish Soap,
1/2 cup Liquid Lawn Food, and
1/2 cup Molasses or Corn Syrup

applied with a 20 gallon hose-end sprayer.

Step 7: To discourage insects and disease, bathe this group every 2 weeks for the rest of the growing season with my All Season "Clean Up" Tonic:

1 cup Liquid Dish Soap,
1 cup Chewing Tobacco Juice, and
1 cup Antiseptic Mouthwash

in your 20 gallon hose-end sprayer, filling the balance of the jar with warm water. If medication is necessary, add fruit tree spray or DURSBAN to this mixture at the recommended rates.

FALL

Step 8: In the snowbelt, never feed this group after August 15th. But you need to encourage root development, so sprinkle this mixture:

1/2 lb. Epsom salts, and
1 cup Paradichlorobenzene crystals

under each tree from the trunk out to the weep line.

🍄 TREES, SHRUBS & EVERGREENS

Step 9: To put this group to bed for the winter, spray them with a mixture of:

**1 can Beer, and
1 cup Liquid Dish Soap**

applied with your 20 gallon hose-end sprayer, filling the balance of the jar with ammonia.

TREE, SHRUB & EVERGREEN TIPS

- Beat your trees in spring with a rolled-up newspaper to stimulate sap flow.
- Dormant spray in early spring and late fall.
- Apply CloudCover® in late spring and early fall.
- Mulch well with shredded bark.
- Seal all cuts or wounds with interior latex paint thinned with antiseptic mouthwash.
- Root prune in October to stimulate next year's growth.

FLOWERS

SPRING

Step 1: Soil buildup is critical! Condition the soil by applying a mixture of:

25 lbs. Garden Food,
10 lbs. Gypsum,
2 lbs. Diatomaceous Earth, and
1 lb. Sugar

with your hand-held broadcast spreader set on the medium setting. Spade the soil deep, then let set for 3 days.

Step 2: Place a thin layer of fresh grass clippings over the spaded area, till it very, very well, then let set for 2 days.

Step 3: Jump start your flower beds by overspraying them with a mixture of:

1 can Beer,
1 cup Liquid Dish Soap,
1 cup Antiseptic Mouthwash, and
1/4 tsp. Instant Tea Granules

in your 20 gallon sprayer, filling the balance of the jar with regular (non-diet) cola. This mixture should be applied to 100 sq. ft. of yarden area. Let the soil set for 2 days.

Step 4: Prepare bulbs, tubers and corms for planting by soaking them in a solution of:

1 can Beer,
2 tbsp. Liquid Dish Soap, and
1/4 tsp. Instant Tea Granules

mixed in 2 gallons of water.

America's Master Gardener®

⚘ FLOWERS

Step 5: Bathe perennials and above-the-ground bulbs with a mixture of:

1 cup Liquid Dish Soap,
1 cup Chewing Tobacco Juice,
1 cup Antiseptic Mouthwash, and
2 drops Tabasco® Sauce

mixed in your 20 gallon hose-end sprayer, filling the balance of the jar with warm water.

Step 6: 10 days after planting, feed your flowers in the morning with my All Season "Green Up" Tonic:

1 can Beer,
1 cup Ammonia,
1/2 cup Liquid Dish Soap,
1/2 cup Liquid Lawn Food, and
1/2 cup Molasses or Corn Syrup

applied with your 20 gallon hose-end sprayer. Feed your flowers every 3 weeks in the morning for the rest of the growing season with this mixture.

SUMMER

Step 7: To discourage insects and disease, bathe your flower beds every 2 weeks, in the evening, for the rest of the growing season, with my All Season "Clean Up" Tonic:

1 cup Liquid Dish Soap,
1 cup Chewing Tobacco Juice, and
1 cup Antiseptic Mouthwash

in your 20 gallon hose-end sprayer, filling the balance of the jar with warm water.

FALL

Step 8: Summer flowering bulbs should be removed, washed in a mild dish soap solution, dried, dusted with medicated foot powder and stored in an old onion or potato bag.

Step 9: Give your fall planted bulbs an organic lunch by mixing:

> **10 lbs. Dehydrated Manure or Compost**
> **5 lbs. Bone Meal**
> **1 lb. Epsom salts**

per 100 sq. ft. of soil. Add up to **15 lbs. of fireplace ashes** to the soil for a real treat.

Step 10: Fall clean-up is a must! Afterwards, overspray your flower beds with a mixture of:

> **1 can Beer,**
> **1 can Regular (non-diet) Cola,**
> **1/2 cup Liquid Dish Soap, and**
> **1/2 cup Chewing Tobacco Juice**

applied with your 20 gallon hose-end sprayer.

Step 11: Cover your flower beds with finely mowed grass clippings and leaves and overspray with a mixture of:

> **1 can Regular (non-diet) Cola,**
> **1 cup Liquid Dish Soap, and**
> **1/4 cup Ammonia**

mixed in your 20 gallon hose-end sprayer, filling the balance of the jar with warm water.

Step 12: 7 to 10 days later, lightly spade in this material and then let set for the winter.

FLOWER TIPS

- Cedar pencil shavings mixed into the soil discourage insects.
- Spray all foliage with CloudCover® in early summer to retain moisture.
- Mulch with grass clippings.
- Pinch, pick or cut flowers often to promote more blooms.
- Plant bulbs in the fall after the first killing frost.

America's / Master Gardener®

VEGETABLES

SPRING

Step 1: Condition the soil in your garden beds as soon as you can by applying a mixture of:

25 lbs. Organic Garden Food,
1 lb. Sugar, and
1/2 lb. Epsom salts

with your hand-held broadcast spreader set on the medium setting.

Step 2: Jump start your garden by overspraying it with a mixture of:

1 can Beer,
1 cup Liquid Dish Soap,
1 cup Antiseptic Mouthwash, and
1/4 tsp. Instant Tea Granules

in your 20 gallon hose-end sprayer, filling the balance of the jar with a regular (non-diet) cola. This mixture should be applied to 100 sq. ft. of yarden area. Let the soil set for 2 days.

SPRING/SUMMER

Step 3: 10 days after planting, feed your garden in the morning with my All Season "Green Up" Tonic:

1 can Beer,
1 cup Ammonia,
1/2 cup Liquid Dish Soap,
1/2 cup Liquid Lawn Food, and
1/2 cup Molasses or Corn Syrup

applied with your 20 gallon hose-end sprayer. Feed your garden with this mixture every 3 weeks, in the morning, for the rest of the growing season.

Step 4: To discourage insects and disease, bathe your garden every 2 weeks, in the evening, for the rest of the growing season, with my All Season "Clean Up" Tonic

1 cup Children's Shampoo,
1 cup Chewing Tobacco Juice, and
1 cup Antiseptic Mouthwash

in your 20 gallon hose-end sprayer, filling the balance of the jar with warm water.

FALL

Step 5: Fall clean up is a must! Afterwards, overspray your garden beds with a mixture of:

1 can Beer,
1 can Regular (non-diet) Cola,
1/2 cup Liquid Dish Soap, and
1/2 cup Chewing Tobacco Juice

applied with your 20 gallon hose-end sprayer.

Step 6: Cover your garden beds with finely mowed grass clippings and leaves, and overspray this debris with a mixture of:

1 can Regular (non-diet) Cola,
1 cup Liquid Dish Soap, and
1/4 cup Ammonia

mixed in your 20 gallon hose-end sprayer, filling the balance of the jar with warm water.

Step 7: 7 to 10 days later, lightly spade in this material and then let set for the winter.

VEGETABLE TIPS

- Plan your garden on paper before your plant.
- Locate your garden in a sunny, well-drained area.
- Plant your garden from east to west, with a wind-break such as corn on the western edge.
- Mulch with grass clippings.
- Use only metal poles to stake up your plants.
- Tie plants up with strips of nylon stocking.
- Harvest your vegetables as soon as they ripen.

ROSES

SPRING

Step 1: Wash newly purchased bare-root rose bushes, roots and all, in a bucket of warm water with the following added:
> **1 tbsp. Liquid Dish Soap, and**
> **1/4 tsp. Liquid Bleach**

Step 2: Before planting, soak bare-root rose bushes in a clean bucket of warm water for about half an hour, with the following added:
> **1 tsp. Liquid Dish Soap,**
> **1 tsp. Ammonia, and**
> **2 tbsp. Clear Corn Syrup**

Step 3: When planting rose bushes, sprinkle a mixture of:
> **75% Bone meal, and**
> **25% Epsom salts**

in the soil, adding 1/2 tsp. sugar for each 4 handsful of the Bone meal/Epsom salts mixture.

Step 4: After planting roses, give each bush 2 cups of the following mixture:
> **1 tsp. Liquid Dish Soap,**
> **1 tsp. Vitamin B-1,**
> **1 tsp. Hydrogen Peroxide, and**
> **1 capful Whiskey**
> **in a 1/2 gallon warm tea water**

Step 5: Before you prune your established rose bushes in the spring, bathe them with my All Season "Clean Up" Tonic:
> **1 cup Liquid Dish Soap,**
> **1 cup Chewing Tobacco Juice, and**
> **1 cup Antiseptic Mouthwash**

mixed in your 20 gallon hose-end sprayer, filling the balance of the jar with warm water. Then bathe them every 2 weeks for the rest of the growing season with this same mixture.

Step 6: Feed your established rose bushes initially in the spring with a mixture of:

> **5 lbs. Garden Food,**
> **1 cup Epsom salts,**
> **1 cup Sugar,**
> **4 Pulverized (dried) Banana Peels, and**
> **2 cups Bone meal**

SUMMER

Step 7: After the initial feeding, feed your rose bushes every 3 weeks in the morning, for the rest of the growing season, with my All Season Tonic:

> **1 can Beer,**
> **1 cup Ammonia,**
> **1/2 cup Liquid Dish Soap,**
> **1/2 cup Liquid Lawn Food, and**
> **1/2 cup Molasses or Corn Syrup**

applied with your 20 gallon hose-end sprayer.

FALL

Step 8: Before you mulch or cover your roses for the winter, bathe them one final time with the Step 5 mixture.

ROSE TIPS

- Buy bargains.
- Plant as soon as you can work the soil.
- Plant in a sunny, bright, well-drained location.
- When planting, place the grafting knot just below soil level.
- Cut your roses to promote more flowers.
- Cut stems just above a 5-leaf cluster. Seal all cuts with nail polish dusted with dirt.

OUTDOOR
House Plants

SPRING

Step 1: When planting any plants, including flowers, small fruit or vegetables in containers, mix 2 cups of bone meal and 6 tbsp. of sugar into the soil. Then dampen the soil with a mixture of:

1 oz. Liquid Lawn Food, and
Vitamin B-1 plant food starter

mixed in a gallon of water.

SUMMER

Step 2: To water your outdoor house plants, make a master mix of fortified water in a 1 gallon milk carton tagged or marked "Plant Food" by adding:

1 tbsp. 15-30-15 Fertilizer,
1/2 tsp. Knox Gelatin,
1/2 tsp. Liquid Dish Soap,
1/2 tsp. Corn Syrup,
1/4 tsp. Tea Granules, and
1 capful Whiskey

filling the balance of the carton with water. Then add 1/2 cup of this mixture to every gallon of water you use to water all of your outdoor house plants.

Step 3: If soil insects are a problem, add DURSBAN at a quarter of the recommended rate to the Step 2 mixture.

Step 4: All house plants should be bathed at least twice a week with a mixture of weak tea (use a twice-used tea bag) in a quart of warm water, adding:

6 drops Liquid Dish Soap,
6 drops Ammonia, and
4 drops Antiseptic Mouthwash

Apply this mixture with a hand sprayer or small compression sprayer.

Step 5: The Step 2 feedings and Step 4 baths should be done before 11:00 a.m. to insure proper ingestion, digestion and comfort for the plants.

FALL

Step 6: Before you bring your plants in for the winter, thoroughly wash them down with a mixture of:

1/4 cup Liquid Dish Soap, and
DURSBAN at the recommended rate

mixed in your 10 gallon hose-end sprayer, filling the balance of the jar with warm water. Let the excess drain through the soil.

Step 7: Let your plants gradually adapt to the indoors by leaving them outdoors during the day, and bringing them indoors at night.

Step 8: Isolate these plants for the first few days so that if pests develop, they can be treated promptly.

OUTDOOR HOUSE PLANT TIPS

- Mulching is a must!
- Spray all plants with CloudCover® in the spring and fall.
- Water outdoor container plants almost every day.
- Move plants back indoors when the temperature drops to 55°F.
- In late fall, wrap the heads of all permanent outdoor plants with burlap.

TONIC
Summary

ALL SEASON "GREEN UP" TONIC

Feed all yarden areas every 3 weeks, in the morning, during the growing season with my All Season "Green Up" Tonic:

1 can Beer,
1 cup Ammonia,
1/2 cup Liquid Dish Soap,
1/2 cup Liquid Lawn Food, and
1/2 cup Molasses or Corn Syrup

applied with your 20 gallon hose-end sprayer.

ALL SEASON "CLEAN UP" TONIC

To discourage insects and prevent disease during the growing season, bathe all yarden areas every 2 weeks, right after you mow, with my All Season "Clean Up" Tonic:

1 cup Liquid Dish Soap,
1 cup Chewing Tobacco Juice,* and
1 cup Antiseptic Mouthwash,

in your 20 gallon hose-end sprayer, filling the balance of the jar with warm water.

*Chewing tobacco juice is made by placing 3 fingers of chewing tobacco in an old nylon stocking and soaking it in a gallon of hot water until the mixture is dark brown.

ASK JERRY

?

If you have a particular lawn, garden or house plant question, why not ask Jerry about it? To get to the root of your problem, please print your question or problem on a postcard and send it to:

Ask Jerry, Box 1001, Wixom, MI 48393.*

QUESTION   **SOLUTION**

_____

_____

_____

_____

_____

_____

_____

_____

_____

_____

_____

_____

_____

_____

*Due to the volume of mail he receives, Jerry can't answer each individual question. He will, however, answer the most frequently asked questions in the "Ask Jerry" column in his "On the Garden Line" newsletter (Item #MAS AO27 – $19.95 per year), so watch for your question and answer there.

Jerry Baker
America's / Master Gardener®

NOTES

Lawns

_____
_____
_____
_____
_____

Trees, Shrubs & Evergreens

_____
_____
_____
_____
_____
_____

Flowers

_____
_____
_____
_____
_____
_____

Vegetables

_____

_____

_____

_____

_____

Roses

_____

_____

_____

_____

_____

_____

House Plants

_____

_____

_____

_____

_____

_____

CONVERSION
Table

MULTIPLY	TO OBTAIN
Feet by 30.48	Centimeters
Feet by .3048	Meters
Gallons by 3.785	Liters
Gallons Water by 8.3453	Lbs. of Water
Inches by 2.540	Centimeters
Meters by 3.281	Feet
Meters by 39.37	Inches
Miles by 1.609	Kilometers
Miles Per Hr. by 1.609	Kilometers Per Hr.
Millimeters by 0.03937	Inches
Ounces by 2	Tablespoons (Liq.)
Ounces by 6	Teaspoons (Liq.)
Ounces by 3	Tablespoons (Dry)
Ounces by 9	Teaspoons (Dry)
Tablespoons (Liq.) by 0.5	Ounces
Tablespoons (Dry) by 0.3333	Ounces
Temp (C) +17.78 by 1.8	Temp (F)
Temp (F) -32 by 5/9	Temp (C)

LIQUID VOLUME EQUIVALENTS

Gal.	Qt.	Pt.	Fl. Oz.	Cups	Tbsp.	Tsp.
1	4	8	128	16		
	1	2	32	4		
		1	16	2	32	
			1	1/8	2	6
				1	16	48
					1	3
						1

TURF MEASUREMENT

1 acre	43,560 sq. ft.